Metro Awakening game guide

Explore, Survive, Conquer and Master Every Challenge

Mac O. Albert

Copyright © 2024 by Mac O. Albert

All rights reserved.

No part of this publication may be reproduced, distributed, or transmitted in any form or by any means, including photocopying, recording, or other electronic or mechanical methods, without the prior written permission of the publisher, except in the case of brief quotations embodied in critical reviews and certain other non-commercial uses permitted by copyright law. For permission requests, write to the publisher at the address below.

Disclaimer

Metro Awakening: The Ultimate Guide is an independent publication and is not affiliated with or endorsed by the developers of *Metro Awakening* or any associated parties. All copyrights, trademarks, and other intellectual property rights related to *Metro Awakening* are owned by their respective copyright holders, including Vertigo Games, the game's publisher, and any other relevant entities.

No Official Affiliation:
This book is not an official strategy guide and is not authorized, sponsored, or endorsed by the creators of *Metro Awakening*. The information contained within is based on the author's personal experience, research, and analysis of the game. All trademarks, brand names, and logos used in this publication are the property of their respective owners.

Accuracy of Information:
While every effort has been made to ensure the accuracy of the information provided in this guide, the author and publisher do not guarantee the completeness or accuracy of the content. Game updates, patches, or modifications may alter gameplay, and strategies, tips, and methods may become outdated. Readers are encouraged to verify information through their own in-game experience and online communities.

Liability Disclaimer:
The author, publisher, and any affiliates are not responsible for any damage to your system, data, or

devices resulting from the use of the advice or instructions in this guide. This includes, but is not limited to, loss of progress, technical issues, or failure to follow gameplay strategies correctly.

Fair Use Notice:
This publication falls under the fair use doctrine and is intended solely for educational, commentary, and informational purposes. All third-party content such as screenshots, logos, and images are used with the understanding that they fall under fair use and are used for the purpose of discussion, criticism, and review.

Reader Responsibility:
By using this guide, readers acknowledge that they are solely responsible for their own gaming experience and decisions. This guide is designed to enhance your gameplay, but the ultimate responsibility for how the game is played rests with the player.

Table of contents

DISCLAIMER 3
1. INTRODUCTION 7
    1.1 Game Overview 7
    1.2 Story and Lore: Setting the Stage for Metro Awakening 8
    1.3 New Gameplay Features and Innovations 9
    1.4 A Prequel to Metro 2033: Understanding the Timeline 11
CHAPTER 2: GETTING STARTED 13
    2.1 First Impressions: The Opening Hours 13
    2.2 Essential Gameplay Mechanics 14
    2.3 Setting Up for Success: Adjusting Settings and Controls 16
    2.4 Navigating the UI and Inventory System 18
CHAPTER 3: PROTAGONIST AND CHARACTERS 20
    3.1 Meet the New Protagonist: Backstory and Abilities 20
    3.2 Supporting Characters: Allies and Enemies 22
    3.3 Character Progression and Skill Trees 24
CHAPTER 4: WALKTHROUGH 27
    4.1 Main Story Mission Overview 27
    4.2 Act I: Early Challenges and Key Objectives 28
    4.3 Act II: Turning Points and Major Decisions 30
    4.4 Act III: The Final Push and Endgame Strategies 32
    4.5 Side Missions and Optional Content 34
CHAPTER 5 CHARACTER DEVELOPMENT AND UPGRADES 35
    5.1 The Protagonist's Skill Tree and Abilities 35
    5.2 How to Manage Gear and Weapon Upgrades 38
    5.3 Optimizing Crafting Materials for Maximum Efficiency 40
    5.4 Tips for Balancing Stealth and Combat Skills 42
CHAPTER 6: EXPLORATION AND ENVIRONMENT 44
    6.1 The World of Metro Awakening: Locations and Layouts 44
    6.2 Key Landmarks and Hidden Secrets 47
    6.3 Navigating the Terrain: Best Practices for Survival 49

    6.4 Resource Management: How to Gather and Use Supplies Effectively 51

CHAPTER 7: EQUIPMENT AND CUSTOMIZATION 53

    7.1 Weapons and Mods: How to Optimize Your Arsenal 53
    7.2 Armor and Protective Gear 57
    7.3 Crafting and Resource Management 59
    7.4 Upgrades and Enhancements: Maximizing Efficiency 61

CHAPTER 8: VR MODE: IMMERSION AND TIPS 63

    8.1 The VR Experience: What to Expect 63
    8.2 Setting Up and Adjusting for VR Play 65
    8.3 Tips for Enhancing VR Gameplay 68
    8.4 Overcoming VR Challenges and Comfort Issues 70

CHAPTER 9: ADVANCED STRATEGIES AND ENDGAME CONTENT 72

    9.1 Maximizing Your Character Build 72
    9.2 Endgame Strategies for the Most Difficult Missions 75
    9.3 Collectibles and Achievements 77
    9.4 New Game+ and Replay Value 78

CHAPTER 10: TROUBLESHOOTING AND FAQS 81

    10.1 Common Issues and Fixes 81
    10.2 Frequently Asked Questions 85

CONCLUSION 89

1. Introduction

1.1 Game Overview

Metro Awakening is the latest entry in the beloved *Metro* series, but with a bold twist that sets it apart from its predecessors. Unlike previous titles, which revolved around the classic *first-person shooter* formula, *Metro Awakening* takes the series into new territory, integrating immersive Virtual Reality (VR) gameplay with the same tension-filled stealth and combat mechanics that fans have come to expect. The game transports players into the chilling, post-apocalyptic world set five years before the events of *Metro 2033*, offering a unique opportunity to experience a fresh narrative in the grim and gritty universe of the Metro.

In this new chapter, players are introduced to a completely new protagonist, one whose personal journey unfolds in the shadow of the disaster that would eventually lead to the world as we know it in the *Metro* series. Set against the backdrop of a decimated Moscow, players must navigate treacherous tunnels, face off against deadly mutants, and make crucial decisions that will shape their survival. With VR capabilities, *Metro Awakening* promises to be an unforgettable experience—one that pulls you right into the heart of the action.

From a visual perspective, the game showcases a stunning, atmospheric world, filled with intricately designed environments that convey a sense of hopelessness and isolation. Every corner of the Metro is alive with detail—whether it's the flickering lights of abandoned stations or the echoes of distant, unseen horrors. The VR aspect, paired with the game's robust physics engine, makes this entry feel more immersive than ever before.

1.2 Story and Lore: Setting the Stage for *Metro Awakening*

The world of *Metro Awakening* is set in a post-apocalyptic Russia, where civilization has crumbled, and only the most resilient survivors have clung to life beneath the surface. The story begins five years before the events of *Metro 2033*, in a world that is still reeling from the initial fallout of the global nuclear war. Though the *Metro* series has always been known for its gripping narrative, *Metro Awakening* raises the stakes by exploring new facets of the universe, shedding light on the origins of key events that would go on to shape the future of the series.

In this prequel, players take on the role of a nameless protagonist—an average citizen who, by circumstance, is forced to become something far more. Without giving too much away, the game intricately explores the early days of the catastrophe, following the protagonist's harrowing journey as they uncover secrets about the war, its devastating aftermath, and the terrifying forces that now haunt the tunnels.

The game's setting is full of haunting, atmospheric locations—from decaying subway stations and hidden bunkers to the wilderness of the irradiated outside world. The lore delves deeper into the factions that populated the Metro before it became the fractured, brutal world players encountered in earlier *Metro* titles. As you venture through these locations, you'll discover logs, journals, and documents that provide a deeper understanding of the world and its inhabitants, offering a narrative rich in mystery and lore.

The game doesn't just focus on survival; it emphasizes the philosophical questions that arise in such a bleak environment. *Metro Awakening* examines what it means to hold onto hope in a world where humanity has almost entirely been wiped out. It challenges the notion of morality in an environment where survival often trumps ethical considerations.

As players progress, they will witness the transformation of this nameless character from an innocent survivor to someone who must make life-altering decisions that affect the future of their group and, possibly, the fate of the Metro. Each step you take into the unknown world of *Metro Awakening* uncovers a new layer of mystery and drama—one that invites you to explore not only the physical world of the Metro but the deeper, philosophical themes of survival, identity, and human nature.

1.3 New Gameplay Features and Innovations

One of the most notable innovations in *Metro Awakening* is its incorporation of Virtual Reality, which brings a new level of immersion to the series. VR allows players to physically experience the horrors of the Metro in a way that previous *Metro* games simply couldn't achieve. The tension of sneaking through dark, enemy-infested tunnels, hearing distant growls echoing off the walls, or suddenly finding yourself face-to-face with a terrifying mutant takes on a whole new meaning in VR. The realism is palpable, creating a sense of dread and suspense that will keep players on the edge of their seats throughout the game.

The game's combat system has also received a major overhaul. While stealth has always been a core component of the *Metro* series, *Metro Awakening* pushes this aspect to the forefront, giving players more tools and options for quietly dealing with threats. Whether it's crafting makeshift weapons, setting traps, or using the environment to your advantage, the game encourages you to think strategically about how you approach each encounter.

Resource management is another aspect of the game that remains central, but it's been expanded with more in-depth systems. Players must scavenge for ammunition, medical supplies, and food, but they also have the opportunity to modify and upgrade their equipment. The ability to craft and repair weapons, armor, and gadgets will be vital to surviving the more dangerous sections of the game. The limited availability of resources adds to the game's sense of tension, forcing players to think carefully about when to fight, when to hide, and when to use precious supplies.

The environmental storytelling in *Metro Awakening* is also more immersive than ever before. As you journey through the Metro, every abandoned station, dark tunnel, and ruined cityscape is a reminder of the world that was lost. Scavenger hunters, remnants of the Russian military, and other survivors all tell their stories through the items they left behind. Each location holds its own secrets, and discovering these pieces of the past adds depth and intrigue to the overall narrative.

In addition, the AI behavior of enemies has been greatly improved. Mutants and hostile survivors now exhibit more realistic, unpredictable reactions, which forces players to constantly adapt their strategies. Gone are the days of scripted enemy movements—now, every interaction feels more dynamic and organic.

The VR experience has also been fine-tuned to ensure it's as intuitive as it is immersive. The developers have worked hard to make sure that the controls are responsive, while still maintaining the same level of difficulty that fans of the series expect. This is not a game that will hold your hand—it's a test of survival and wit, designed to challenge even the most experienced gamers.

1.4 A Prequel to Metro 2033: Understanding the Timeline

For long-time fans of the *Metro* series, the timeline of *Metro Awakening* will hold a particular significance. As a prequel to *Metro 2033*, the game sheds light on the early days of the Metro and the events that led to the grim future seen in the original title. While *Metro 2033* focused on the protagonist Artyom's journey through a post-apocalyptic world where humanity was on the brink of extinction, *Metro Awakening* dives into the crucial moments that preceded this downfall.

The events of *Metro Awakening* show the world as it began to fall apart. The devastation caused by nuclear war, the early stages of the outbreak of mutants, and the formation of the underground factions that would play pivotal roles in the later *Metro* games are all explored. These events help to contextualize the broader world that Artyom and his fellow survivors inhabit in *Metro 2033* and beyond.

Understanding this timeline is essential for appreciating the full scope of *Metro Awakening*. The game ties directly into the established lore of the series, giving players new insight into familiar locations and characters while introducing new narratives that will leave them wondering about the future of the franchise.

As a prequel, *Metro Awakening* offers an exciting opportunity to explore the events that shaped the Metro universe. It allows players to see how the world began its descent into the harsh reality depicted in the *Metro* series, providing both new and old fans with a deeper understanding of the overarching storyline.

Chapter 2: Getting Started

2.1 First Impressions: The Opening Hours

When you first launch *Metro Awakening*, the experience immediately captivates you with its atmospheric tension and immersive VR world-building. From the moment you step into the shoes of the new protagonist, you are thrust into a desolate, ravaged world—completely void of any light except for the faint glow from crumbling city structures. The first few hours are designed to hook you into the game's gritty universe, offering a slow and methodical introduction to its mechanics, storytelling, and survival elements. If you're a *Metro* veteran, the feeling will be familiar, but it'll still be fresh enough to surprise you.

The Visuals:
As you adjust to the immersive VR setting, you'll notice the level of detail that went into crafting the game's environments. From the decayed subway tunnels to the desolate open world, *Metro Awakening* doesn't shy away from showing you the impact of the apocalypse on the cityscape. The textures are rich and realistic, and the sound design is absolutely top-notch, creating a level of immersion that will have you feeling like you're standing in the midst of a desolate, crumbling world.

Introduction to Gameplay:
The first hours of gameplay ease you into the mechanics. You'll start with basic movement controls, learning how to interact with objects in the environment, pick up weapons, and engage in combat. The game introduces you to your character's abilities slowly, ensuring you understand the core mechanics of stealth, resource management, and combat before throwing you into the heat of battle.

For newcomers to the *Metro* series, the pacing will feel deliberate, but there's always something that pushes you forward—a tense atmosphere or an unexpected event that keeps you hooked. Don't be surprised if you find yourself carefully exploring every corner, searching for collectibles and resources. The game encourages this type of exploration from the start, allowing you to learn the lay of the land before the stakes are raised higher.

2.2 Essential Gameplay Mechanics

Metro Awakening brings a fresh take on the familiar gameplay mechanics of the *Metro* series. As an expert in the genre, I'll Walk you through some of the essential mechanics you'll need to master to survive in this unforgiving world.

Stealth Combat:
One of the most defining features of the *Metro* series is its stealth-based gameplay. *Metro Awakening* builds on this with more intricate and engaging stealth mechanics, especially when playing in VR. You'll need to carefully avoid enemy detection by staying in the shadows, moving

silently, and using distractions. But beware—enemies are quick to react if they notice something amiss, and sometimes it's better to just take cover and wait for them to pass.

To execute stealth attacks, you'll need to crouch and sneak up on enemies. The use of silenced weapons, such as pistols or crossbows, will help you avoid alerting nearby threats. As you progress, the game will also introduce you to the ability to distract enemies using items you find in the world—whether that's throwing a bottle to lure enemies away or using an EMP to disable electronic surveillance systems.

Resource Management:
Survival is a key theme in *Metro Awakening*, and managing resources will be critical to your success. Ammo, food, medical supplies, and crafting materials are all finite, and you'll need to be mindful of how and when you use them. At times, you may find yourself running low on bullets, so it's essential to make use of melee combat when possible, or to engage in risky but rewarding exploration to find hidden caches of supplies.

The game also introduces a crafting system where you can create your own ammunition, traps, and other useful tools, depending on what you've scavenged. The scarcity of supplies will keep you on edge, and it's often better to err on the side of caution and ration what you have. When you first start, don't rush through areas too quickly. Take your time to gather materials, check every corner, and explore side areas for hidden resources.

Weapon and Equipment Customization:
Unlike previous *Metro* games, *Metro Awakening* offers deeper customization options for weapons and equipment. As you collect weapons, you'll also find various upgrade parts—suppressors, scopes, barrels, and stocks—that can enhance your gear. The game encourages experimentation with different setups. For example, you might opt for a faster-firing weapon with less accuracy, or a slower, more powerful weapon with precision, depending on your playstyle. In VR, the customization options feel more hands-on, as you physically adjust weapon components with your hands in the virtual world.

Health and Stamina:
Your character's health is crucial, and it's easy to get overwhelmed if you're not careful. The game introduces a stamina mechanic, which means running, climbing, and engaging in combat all drain your stamina. When this happens, your character becomes more vulnerable, so you'll need to keep an eye on how much energy you're expending. Managing your health is also critical—keeping an eye out for medkits and healing items will be essential, as you'll often face situations where health packs are few and far between.

2.3 Setting Up for Success: Adjusting Settings and Controls

Before diving deep into *Metro Awakening*, it's essential to adjust the game's settings and controls to ensure that you're as comfortable and prepared as possible. Since the game is designed for VR, the settings menu offers a wide range of options tailored for both comfort and performance.

1. VR Comfort Settings:
The immersive nature of VR means that comfort is crucial. You'll want to fine-tune settings to reduce motion sickness and optimize your experience. Start by adjusting the comfort settings in the VR menu. Options like "Snap Turn" and "Smooth Turn" can significantly affect how you experience the game. If you're new to VR, you may want to start with snap turning (which limits the amount of turn per movement) and gradually increase to smooth turning as you get used to the immersion.

Another setting to experiment with is the "Field of View" (FOV). A higher FOV can reduce the feeling of tunnel vision, but it might make some elements in the game feel more distant. If you're experiencing discomfort or dizziness, a lower FOV can help.

2. Audio Settings:
The sound design in *Metro Awakening* is integral to the experience. The atmospheric audio will pull you into the world, while the crisp sounds of enemy movements, footsteps, and environmental hazards will keep you on your toes. Make sure to set the volume levels to your liking, and consider using headphones for the most immersive experience. You can also adjust the balance between ambient sound and voice dialogue, ensuring that you can hear both clearly while staying immersed in the game's world.

3. Control Layout:
Adjusting the control layout is also an important step. VR games can sometimes have a steep learning curve when it comes to controls, but *Metro Awakening* offers an intuitive layout that should feel natural once you get used to it. If you're struggling with certain actions, such as aiming or reloading, consider tweaking the button mapping to suit your preferences. You can also adjust sensitivity settings for movement and combat to find the ideal balance between responsiveness and control.

4. Visual Settings:
Finally, tweak the visual settings for optimal performance. If you have a high-end VR system, you'll want to push the graphical settings to the maximum to enjoy the best visuals. However, if your system is more mid-range, adjusting the resolution or turning off some advanced graphical effects can ensure smoother gameplay. Be mindful of frame rates—low FPS can lead to discomfort in VR, so keeping the frame rate at a consistent 60 FPS or higher is crucial for maintaining immersion and comfort.

2.4 Navigating the UI and Inventory System

The user interface (UI) and inventory system in *Metro Awakening* are designed with ease of use in mind, even in the virtual world. The VR format allows for a more immersive interaction with your inventory, weapons, and resources.

1. The Inventory Menu:
Instead of using a traditional on-screen menu, *Metro Awakening* employs a virtual inventory system. By reaching out with your hand, you'll access a floating inventory menu, allowing you to examine your gear, swap weapons, and manage your resources. This system feels intuitive in VR, as you physically reach for and manipulate your items in the environment. The inventory is organized into categories, such as weapons, medical supplies, and crafting materials, making it easy to quickly find what you need during tense moments.

2. Weapon Wheel:
To equip or swap weapons, you can use a radial wheel. This can be accessed by holding a button or gesture, allowing you to cycle through your available weapons quickly. As you collect more weapons, the wheel can get a bit crowded, so it's helpful to assign your most-used weapons to easily accessible spots. A good strategy is to keep a close-range weapon (like a knife or pistol) for stealth situations and a more powerful long-range weapon for combat.

3. Environmental Interaction:
Beyond weapons and health items, the game's interface allows you to interact with the environment in meaningful ways. This includes opening lockers, picking up items, and using tools like the flashlight or gas mask. Your hand motions are directly mapped to these actions, so you'll need to be comfortable with the VR controls to navigate smoothly through the environment.

Chapter 3: Protagonist and Characters

3.1 Meet the New Protagonist: Backstory and Abilities

In *Metro Awakening*, the story pivots on an entirely new protagonist—a character whose history and skills are crucial to the narrative's development. Unlike Artyom from the earlier *Metro* titles, this new hero is introduced with a fresh backstory that provides both mystery and motivation. The protagonist, who we'll refer to as **Alexei**, is a survivor from a hidden enclave of people living beneath the remnants of a decimated city. His early life is marked by hardships, having lost his family to the mutant horrors that plague the surface world. Raised in the remnants of the metro tunnels, Alexei is forged by an unrelenting world where survival often comes at the cost of compassion.

Backstory and Motivation:
Alexei's journey begins as a simple scout tasked with gathering resources for his underground community. However, a mission gone wrong leads him into a labyrinth of mystery and treachery, where he uncovers secrets that could change the fate of humanity. What's interesting about Alexei's story is how it ties into the broader *Metro*

lore without requiring prior knowledge of previous games. He's a man marked by loss but driven by a desire to uncover the truth about the events that led to the world's downfall.

Abilities:
As a skilled scout and tracker, Alexei's abilities are rooted in stealth, agility, and survival. Unlike Artyom's more brute-force approach in earlier titles, Alexei's strength lies in his adaptability. He has the ability to read enemy movements and use the environment to his advantage. For example, his proficiency with low-light vision helps him move undetected in dark areas, and his keen hearing allows him to pick up on faint sounds—perfect for avoiding traps and sneaky enemies.

Alexei also possesses a unique skillset called "Environmental Camouflage," which is particularly useful in VR mode. By blending into his surroundings, he can avoid combat or set up ambushes. This ability plays a crucial role in the game's stealth mechanics and adds an extra layer of depth to the overall gameplay.

VR Integration and Realism:
One of the most striking features of Alexei's abilities is how well they integrate into the VR experience. Each action feels highly tactile and immersive, as you must physically crouch or lean to take advantage of cover or peek around corners. It's these small, subtle actions that make playing *Metro Awakening* in VR feel unlike any other game in the series. You won't just be pressing a button to hide behind a wall—you'll physically move your body, adding to the immersion and challenge.

3.2 Supporting Characters: Allies and Enemies

While Alexei is the centerpiece of *Metro Awakening*, the game wouldn't be the same without its diverse cast of allies and enemies, each adding depth to the story and enhancing the gameplay experience.

Allies:
Throughout the game, Alexei forms bonds with several key characters, each of whom plays a pivotal role in his journey. One of the most notable allies is **Kira**, a former military officer who now acts as a guide in the dangerous, irradiated wastelands. Kira is the embodiment of resilience. Her backstory is rooted in loyalty and survival; she once led a group of soldiers that was decimated by a powerful mutant attack. Her knowledge of combat, strategy, and the ever-changing environment proves invaluable to Alexei.

Kira's character is fully realized through dialogue choices and side missions, which helps build a genuine sense of camaraderie. The interactions between Alexei and Kira are not just based on combat but on emotional growth. As you progress through the game, you'll see them grow together, each learning from the other.

Another key character is **Mikhail**, a grizzled veteran who has survived countless battles against both mutants and human adversaries. Mikhail is less a mentor and more a reluctant partner. His combat skills are unmatched, and his cynicism about the world's future provides a stark contrast to Alexei's hopeful idealism. The tension between these two characters is a major driving force in the narrative, as Mikhail often pushes Alexei toward harder decisions.

On the other hand, **Vera**, a mysterious figure from Alexei's past, reappears mid-game with crucial information about a potential cure for the virus that has ravaged humanity. Vera's enigmatic nature keeps players guessing—her motivations are unclear, but her actions suggest she might have an agenda of her own.

Enemies:
The enemies in *Metro Awakening* are as diverse and complex as the game's protagonists. While mutants remain a constant threat in the desolate world, human enemies—factions of raiders, rogue soldiers, and remnants of military units—also play a significant role in the narrative.

One of the most terrifying new enemies is **The Watchers**, a group of mutated creatures that blend in with the environment. These enemies are particularly dangerous because they can remain nearly invisible, only revealing themselves when they strike. Their stealth abilities require Alexei to remain constantly vigilant, using his hearing and stealth skills to avoid being caught off guard.

Another enemy faction is **The Scavengers**, a ruthless group of survivors who have turned to raiding settlements for supplies. The Scavengers represent a more human threat, forcing players to confront the moral dilemma of fighting other survivors for the sake of their own survival. These encounters aren't just about combat—they often test Alexei's values, as the player must decide whether to kill or negotiate with the human foes they encounter.

Lastly, *Metro Awakening* introduces **The Omega**, a mysterious and powerful antagonist whose identity is revealed late in the game. The Omega represents a darker, more sinister force in the game, manipulating events from the shadows. Encountering The Omega and its followers creates a palpable sense of unease and culminates in one of the most intense final acts in the *Metro* series.

3.3 Character Progression and Skill Trees

One of the standout features of *Metro Awakening* is its comprehensive character progression system, which allows players to tailor Alexei's abilities to fit their preferred playstyle. As Alexei navigates the harsh environments, encounters dangerous foes, and builds relationships with allies, he gains experience points that can be used to enhance his skills.

The Skill Tree:
The skill tree in *Metro Awakening* is divided into three main branches: **Survival**, **Combat**, and **Stealth**. Each branch focuses on a specific aspect of Alexei's abilities, allowing players to specialize in one area or develop a more balanced skillset.

- **Survival**: This branch focuses on improving Alexei's ability to scavenge and survive in the harsh world.

It enhances his resourcefulness, such as crafting better tools and healing items, and boosts his endurance to allow him to survive longer in hazardous environments.

- **Combat**: The Combat branch improves Alexei's prowess in direct combat, such as faster reload times, better accuracy, and stronger attacks. Investing in this tree is crucial for those who prefer a more aggressive approach to gameplay, as it makes Alexei a more formidable opponent in battle.

- **Stealth**: This is where Alexei's tactical and covert abilities shine. The Stealth branch enhances his ability to remain undetected, move silently, and set traps for enemies. For players who prefer to sneak past threats rather than engage head-on, this skill tree provides essential upgrades.

As players progress through the game, they will be able to unlock and upgrade various abilities within these skill trees. The choices made in the progression system significantly impact gameplay, allowing players to experiment with different strategies. For example, focusing heavily on Stealth allows Alexei to bypass enemies entirely, whereas an emphasis on Combat makes him a powerhouse in firefights.

Skill Points and Crafting:
Skill points are earned by completing story missions, side quests, and overcoming significant challenges. The game also introduces a crafting system where Alexei can

combine various materials to create useful items like traps, explosives, and equipment upgrades. These crafted items, combined with his skill tree abilities, create a dynamic and flexible gameplay experience.

Each decision in the progression system feels meaningful. Players must carefully consider their choices, as they will shape the way Alexei interacts with the world and tackles challenges. Want to focus on mastering long-range weapons and traps? Or would you prefer to slip through the shadows undetected? The choice is yours.

Chapter 4: Walkthrough

4.1 Main Story Mission Overview

The central narrative of *Metro Awakening* takes place in a post-apocalyptic world, with a unique storyline that introduces new characters, settings, and plotlines. Unlike other titles in the *Metro* series, this game's story places a significant emphasis on the new protagonist's personal growth and their role in a wider conflict that affects not just the immediate survivors but the very future of humanity.

The game opens with a brutal reminder of the world's decline. The protagonist finds themselves stranded in a devastated urban environment, surrounded by hostile forces, wild creatures, and scarce resources. The opening sequence sets the tone: survival is not just about defeating enemies but also about understanding the landscape, managing scarce resources, and navigating morally grey decisions.

As you progress through the main storyline, you will encounter pivotal moments that shape the narrative. The story arcs are split into three primary acts, each introducing major challenges and shifting the protagonist's understanding of the world.

4.2 Act I: Early Challenges and Key Objectives

The Beginning of the Journey
Act I begins with a frantic opening sequence that sets the stage for the protagonist's journey. You start in a small, isolated shelter, trying to make sense of the chaos that surrounds you. Right away, the game introduces you to the core mechanics: stealth, exploration, resource management, and combat. Early on, you'll learn how to scavenge for supplies, craft makeshift weapons, and evade dangerous enemies. These skills will be crucial throughout the game.

Key Objectives in Act I:

- **Establishing the First Safe Zone**: Your primary goal in Act I is to make your way to a nearby safe house, which will serve as your base of operations. Along the way, you'll encounter various enemies, from mutant creatures to hostile factions. The game teaches you how to handle stealth, as combat should be approached cautiously at this early stage.

- **Learning to Survive in the Wasteland**: The protagonist's first major challenge is to gather essential supplies—food, medical kits, and ammunition—while also staying alert to environmental dangers like radiation zones or unpredictable weather changes.

- **Introduction to the Story**: During your exploration, you'll encounter your first few characters that help set the tone for the overarching story. These characters will provide insight into the protagonist's backstory, the world they inhabit, and the mysterious threats looming over the horizon.

Key Challenges in Act I:

- **Combat Training**: Early on, combat can feel overwhelming, especially when you're still learning how to handle different weapon types and your first encounters with hostile enemies. The key here is patience—learn to stealthily approach threats, use cover effectively, and only engage in combat when absolutely necessary.

- **Limited Resources**: Resources are scarce in the early stages of the game, and you will often find yourself making tough choices about what to take with you and what to leave behind. Prioritize medical supplies and ammunition, but don't neglect crafting materials for building traps and makeshift weapons.

- **Environmental Hazards**: The world of *Metro Awakening* is unforgiving, and the environmental challenges in Act I introduce players to the dangers of the wasteland. From toxic rain to radioactive zones, players must constantly stay vigilant about the elements, as even the environment itself can become a deadly enemy.

4.3 Act II: Turning Points and Major Decisions

A Shift in Direction

Act II is where the game truly begins to expand, both in terms of gameplay and narrative. The protagonist's journey takes on new dimensions, as they are forced to make critical decisions that will have far-reaching consequences. The story broadens to include a larger cast of characters and introduces factions vying for control of the wasteland.

At the heart of Act II lies the discovery of a powerful artifact—an object that holds the key to the survival of humanity. This artifact becomes the central focus of both the protagonist's quest and the game's plot. While the artifact promises salvation, it also brings danger, as numerous factions and enemies seek to control it for their own purposes.

Key Objectives in Act II:

- **The Artifact's Power**: As you uncover more about the artifact's origins, you learn that it has the potential to either save or doom what remains of civilization. You'll face numerous moral dilemmas—will you protect it at all costs, or will you choose to destroy it to prevent its abuse?
- **Alliances and Betrayals**: Act II is when you'll meet several factions that offer their own brand of aid. Some want to use the artifact for a noble cause,

while others are bent on exploiting its power for dominance. Deciding who to trust becomes one of the game's defining elements in this act. The choices you make here will shape the narrative and gameplay for the rest of the story.

- **New Abilities and Equipment**: By the time Act II rolls around, you will have mastered basic survival techniques. This section of the game allows you to expand your character's abilities and upgrade your equipment, making you a more formidable force. You'll gain access to new skills, better weapons, and more powerful tools to aid in your journey.

Key Challenges in Act II:

- **Moral Dilemmas**: The protagonist's decision-making becomes more complex as you navigate the political intrigue between rival factions. The decisions you make in Act II will often have unexpected consequences, forcing you to confront your own values and beliefs.

- **Tougher Combat**: Enemies become more dangerous and intelligent in Act II, requiring you to use advanced tactics and strategies to overcome them. Whether it's a group of human adversaries with superior weapons or mutated creatures that hunt in packs, the combat challenges are significantly ramped up.

- **Environmental Complexity**: Act II introduces new environmental obstacles, such as high-tech enemy fortifications and expansive urban zones filled with hidden threats. Mastering the game's exploration mechanics is key, as you will need to navigate through tight spaces, avoid traps, and make use of your surroundings to outwit your enemies.

4.4 Act III: The Final Push and Endgame Strategies

The Climax of the Journey
Act III marks the conclusion of the protagonist's journey, with the stakes higher than ever. With the artifact's true power now revealed, you find yourself at the heart of a desperate struggle for control. The narrative reaches its climax as the protagonist must decide whether to use the artifact to reshape the world or to destroy it to prevent a new reign of terror.

This act is where the culmination of your choices in Acts I and II comes to bear. Every decision you've made up to this point plays a role in shaping the finale. The game becomes a race against time, as enemies grow more desperate and the world's resources dwindle even further.

Key Objectives in Act III:

- **The Final Battle for Control**: The ultimate conflict in Act III is about securing the artifact and deciding its fate. This is where the game's most intense combat sequences take place, as the protagonist must confront a unified enemy force that has been built up over the course of the game. Strategic use of all your abilities, weapons, and environmental advantages is key to survival.

- **Resolution of the Moral Dilemma**: The decision you make regarding the artifact will not only affect the ending but also define the future of the wasteland. Whether you choose to use it to bring peace or destroy it to prevent its corruption, your decision will be the final act in the protagonist's journey.

- **Endgame Challenges**: With the story nearing its conclusion, Act III introduces some of the game's toughest challenges. You'll face off against elite enemies, navigate complex environments, and tackle final puzzles that will test everything you've learned throughout the game.

Key Challenges in Act III:

- **Final Boss Fights**: As is common in *Metro* titles, the final act includes some of the game's toughest boss battles. These encounters are designed to push all your combat and tactical skills to the limit. Preparation is key, as you will need to make the most of your upgraded weapons, supplies, and special abilities.

- **Resource Scarcity**: By Act III, resources are even more limited, adding an extra layer of challenge to the game. Every bullet, medkit, and crafting material will be essential, forcing you to make strategic choices about when to fight and when to retreat.

- **Multiple Endings**: Your choices throughout the game will lead to different endings, each offering a unique perspective on the protagonist's journey. Whether you save the world or doom it, the conclusion is satisfying and thought-provoking.

4.5 Side Missions and Optional Content

While the main story is gripping and rich with narrative, *Metro Awakening* also offers a wealth of side missions and optional content to expand your experience.

These side missions allow you to explore more of the world, interact with secondary characters, and uncover hidden stories that deepen your understanding of the *Metro* universe. Some side quests are straightforward and reward you with useful items, while others delve into the backstory of the world's remaining inhabitants, providing emotional depth and offering fresh perspectives on the narrative.

Optional content in *Metro Awakening* can range from simple scavenger hunts to complex multi-step quests that involve solving intricate puzzles or defeating powerful enemies. Completing side missions is not only rewarding but also essential for those who want to maximize their character's potential and fully experience all the game has to offer.

Chapter 5 Character Development and Upgrades

In *Metro Awakening*, the journey to survival is not just about navigating through hostile environments and surviving combat encounters—it's also about evolving as a character. From upgrading your protagonist's skills to carefully managing gear and crafting resources, the development system in this game is crucial to success. To help you get the most out of every element, this section breaks down the key areas of character development and offers actionable advice on how to progress efficiently. Whether you are focused on improving your combat prowess, refining your stealth abilities, or making the most of your crafting materials, this guide provides essential information for mastering every aspect of the game.

5.1 The Protagonist's Skill Tree and Abilities

In *Metro Awakening*, the protagonist's progression is defined by a comprehensive skill tree system. As you progress through the game, you will accumulate experience points (XP) that can be spent to unlock a range of abilities that enhance the protagonist's performance in combat, stealth, and survival. These abilities are divided into distinct categories, allowing players to specialize in different playstyles or create a versatile character that can adapt to any situation.

Understanding the Skill Categories

The skill tree is divided into several categories, each corresponding to a key aspect of the protagonist's development. These categories are:

1. **Combat**
   This category enhances your ability to engage enemies head-on, with upgrades to weapon handling, damage output, and stamina. Key abilities in this category include faster reload speeds, increased damage with melee weapons, and improved accuracy with ranged weapons. If you prefer a more aggressive, direct approach to combat, focusing on the Combat skill tree is essential.

2. **Stealth**
   The Stealth category is perfect for players who prefer to avoid direct confrontation. Upgrades here will improve your ability to remain undetected, move silently, and take down enemies quietly. Some of the notable abilities include faster movement when crouched, the ability to hold breath longer when aiming silently, and enhanced awareness of enemy patrol patterns.

3. **Survival**
   The Survival category is all about improving your ability to handle the harsh environment of the Metro. This skill set enhances your durability,

resistance to environmental hazards, and the efficiency of your health regeneration. Notable upgrades here include reduced damage from environmental factors like radiation and toxic gas, better stamina recovery, and the ability to heal faster using crafted materials.

4. **Crafting**

    Crafting is one of the game's core features, and the Crafting skill tree allows you to improve the effectiveness of the resources you collect. Upgrades in this category will enable you to craft more efficient supplies, such as stronger ammunition, healing items, and even traps. Crafting-focused players will want to prioritize this tree to maximize their resource management and survival chances.

Maximizing Skill Progression

The key to optimizing your protagonist's skill tree is understanding your preferred playstyle. If you are the type of player who enjoys tactical combat, focusing on the Combat skill tree early on will increase your offensive capabilities. For those who prefer to sneak through the shadows, unlocking Stealth upgrades will make your journey easier and safer. However, no matter your approach, a balanced combination of skills will give you the flexibility to adapt to different situations.

As you level up, ensure that you spend your XP on abilities that complement your current needs. For example, if you find yourself often running low on supplies, investing in the Crafting skill tree will allow you to make the most out of your collected materials. On the other hand, if combat feels like a struggle, prioritize combat upgrades until you can handle enemies more effectively.

5.2 How to Manage Gear and Weapon Upgrades

In *Metro Awakening*, weapons and gear are essential for survival. Whether you're facing mutated creatures or hostile factions, having the right tools at your disposal can make or break an encounter. The game provides an array of weapons and gear, each with unique strengths and weaknesses. However, their effectiveness depends on how well you upgrade and manage them.

Weapon Upgrades

One of the most important aspects of your gear management is upgrading weapons. The weapons in *Metro Awakening* are customizable, and you can modify them with various attachments and components that improve performance. These upgrades include scopes, suppressors, extended magazines, and grip enhancements. Weapon upgrades are crucial to making sure your arsenal stays effective as you progress through increasingly difficult challenges.

To upgrade weapons, you will need specific resources—often found through exploration, looting, or by trading with NPCs. Here are some tips for managing weapon upgrades:

- **Prioritize Versatile Weapons**: When starting out, focus on upgrading weapons that can be used in a variety of situations. A versatile weapon, like a modified assault rifle, can handle both long-range and close-quarters combat, making it invaluable throughout the game.

- **Adapt to the Enemy**: Different enemies will require different strategies. Upgrading a shotgun with a tighter spread for close combat or adding a suppressor to your pistol for stealth kills are all important decisions. Understanding the type of enemy, you're facing will guide your upgrade priorities.

- **Craft for Your Weapons**: As you progress through the game, you will also encounter blueprints that allow you to craft specific weapon upgrades. Make sure to prioritize crafting materials that will be most useful for your weapon loadouts, especially those that improve accuracy, rate of fire, or damage output.

Managing Gear

Gear management is also an essential part of surviving in *Metro Awakening*. The game features a variety of armor and utility items that help you endure the hostile world. Managing these items, such as gas masks, armor vests, and healing supplies, is critical.

- **Gas Masks and Filters**: Gas masks are essential for surviving in toxic environments. Filters are required to keep your gas mask functional, and they can be found in various locations. Be mindful of your filter usage, especially when exploring heavily contaminated areas. Upgrading your gas mask to extend the life of your filters will save you valuable resources.

- **Armor**: Upgrading your armor provides increased protection from enemy attacks. You'll find different types of armor throughout the game, each with varying degrees of protection. Prioritize armor upgrades that fit your combat style—light armor for stealth or heavy armor for direct combat.

- **Health Kits and Consumables**: Health kits and other consumable items play a vital role in keeping you alive. Always ensure you have a stockpile of medical supplies, but also focus on crafting efficient healing items to conserve resources. Learn to combine crafting and scavenging to always have a steady supply of health-restoring items.

5.3 Optimizing Crafting Materials for Maximum Efficiency

Crafting is one of the game's most rewarding mechanics, but it's also one of the most resource-intensive. As you explore the world of *Metro Awakening*, you'll come across a variety of materials that can be used to craft everything from ammunition to health items. Efficiently managing these materials will ensure that you are always prepared for whatever the game throws at you.

Crafting Basics

At its core, crafting in *Metro Awakening* revolves around gathering resources and combining them to create useful items. Resources such as scrap metal, chemicals, wood, and fabric are commonly found in the game world. You'll need a crafting table or workbench to combine these materials into usable items.

To optimize your crafting efforts:

- **Prioritize Ammunition**: Ammo is a finite resource, and running out at the wrong moment can leave you vulnerable. Focus on crafting ammo for your primary weapons, ensuring that you always have a supply on hand. Stockpiling ammo early in the game will give you a significant advantage.

- **Craft Multi-Purpose Items**: Some items, like explosives, can be used for multiple purposes—whether for combat, distraction, or solving environmental puzzles. Focus on crafting versatile items that can serve more than one purpose, reducing the number of resources you need to gather.

- **Upgrade Crafting Stations**: Throughout the game, you will encounter crafting stations where you can combine materials. Some of these stations are upgradable, allowing you to craft more complex and powerful items. Upgrade these stations as soon as possible to increase your crafting options.

Resource Management

Resource management is crucial, as the world of *Metro Awakening* doesn't always provide an abundance of materials. Learning how to effectively scavenge for materials and craft only when necessary, can help you conserve valuable resources.

- **Loot Thoroughly**: Make sure to search every nook and cranny for materials. Scavenge in abandoned buildings, enemy outposts, and wreckage for valuable crafting supplies.

- **Trade Wisely**: NPCs offer valuable trades, but make sure you're not overpaying for items you can find easily. Save your barter points for rare items or blueprints that can significantly improve your gear.

5.4 Tips for Balancing Stealth and Combat Skills

In *Metro Awakening*, players are constantly forced to make a choice between stealth and direct combat. The game offers a range of ways to deal with threats—either through sneaky tactics or all-out combat. Balancing these two elements is key to surviving in the world of the game.

Mastering Stealth

Stealth is often the safest and most efficient way to deal with enemies, but it requires careful planning. Stealth-focused players should aim to:

Use Cover Effectively: Always move from cover to cover and stay out of sight. Pay attention to enemy patrol patterns and avoid open areas.

Distract Enemies: Use distractions like throwing rocks or using certain gadgets to divert enemy attention. This can provide you with a window to sneak past them or set up an ambush. Timing is key when using distractions, as they can be more effective if the enemy is already on alert.

Avoiding Detection: Stealth is a huge part of survival in *Indiana Jones and the Great Circle*. Keep your movements slow and deliberate to avoid making noise. Stay in shadows and behind cover, and avoid walking on noisy surfaces like glass or metal. If you can, sneak up on enemies from behind and take them out quietly.

Leverage Environmental Hazards: Many levels feature environmental hazards, such as collapsing bridges, traps, or electrified water. Use these to your advantage to eliminate or incapacitate enemies. For example, lead enemies into traps or lure them into danger to thin out their ranks.

Understand Enemy Patterns: Each enemy type has a set of behaviors and patterns. Some will patrol an area, while others may be stationary. Understanding these patterns allows you to predict their movements and plan your next steps accordingly. Always be patient, and wait for the perfect moment to strike.

Chapter 6: Exploration and Environment

In *Metro Awakening*, the world is as much a character as the protagonist. The game's atmospheric design, environmental storytelling, and the vast, interconnected landscapes all work together to create an immersive and challenging experience. Whether you are sneaking through dark underground tunnels, fighting off dangerous mutated creatures, or scavenging for supplies in the dilapidated remnants of civilization, the environment plays a critical role in shaping your journey.

The game's environments are meticulously crafted, offering players a mix of hostile terrain, hidden secrets, and immersive locales. Mastering the art of exploration is essential, not only for survival but also for uncovering the mysteries of the world around you.

6.1 The World of Metro Awakening: Locations and Layouts

The world of *Metro Awakening* is a blend of dense urban environments, abandoned industrial zones, radioactive wastelands, and underground metro systems. As the first *Metro* title to embrace VR fully, the game heightens the sense of scale and immersion, allowing you to explore these diverse areas in breathtaking detail. Each location is designed to feel like a lived-in world, rich with history and secrets waiting to be uncovered.

Key Locations in Metro Awakening

1. **The Metro Tunnels**: The heart of the game's world lies in the underground metro system. These tunnels, once a bustling lifeline for civilization, are now home to dangers, both natural and man-made. The layout of the metro is labyrinthine, with different districts connecting through various routes, stations, and maintenance tunnels. Some areas are heavily contaminated, requiring careful management of your gas mask filters, while others may feature remnants of human life—desolate but hauntingly beautiful in their abandonment.

2. **The Wasteland**: Above ground, the world is even more hostile. The wasteland is a sprawling, open area where the remnants of cities lie in ruin, ravaged by environmental catastrophes and the remnants of war. The terrain here is often filled with dangerous mutants and hostile factions. With radiation levels fluctuating, survival depends on your ability to find shelter and clean water, as well as scavenging for supplies.

3. **Abandoned Urban Centers**: These large, overgrown cities are relics of the pre-apocalypse world. Tall skyscrapers and shattered windows stand as grim monuments to humanity's downfall. Exploring these cities feels like stepping into a forgotten world, with lootable buildings, dangerous

wreckage, and plenty of hidden pathways that lead to important resources or rare collectibles.

4. **Underground Research Facilities**: For a touch of mystery and science fiction, there are hidden research facilities scattered across the world. These high-tech ruins contain remnants of experiments and advanced technology, offering unique rewards but also hiding formidable enemies. The atmospheric tension in these places is palpable—creaking floors, malfunctioning lights, and ominous sounds that make every corner feel like a potential danger zone.

5. **Safe Havens and Encampments**: While much of the world is perilous, there are places of relative safety. These are temporary respites where survivors gather, trade, and attempt to make sense of the chaos. Some of these camps are friendly, offering useful resources, while others may harbor dark secrets or be rife with conflict. Engaging with these enclaves is vital for replenishing your supplies, gaining valuable intel, and advancing the story.

Understanding the Layout

Navigating the world of *Metro Awakening* requires more than just a map—it requires an understanding of its layout. Many areas are interconnected, with underground tunnels leading to seemingly unrelated locations. As you explore, you'll discover shortcuts, hidden passages, and alternate routes that allow you to bypass enemies or avoid dangerous zones. The game encourages a non-linear exploration approach, allowing you to chart your own course and uncover secrets at your own pace.

Exploring these vast areas requires paying close attention to environmental cues. Look for signs of previous human activity, such as old signs, graffiti, or personal belongings that hint at the history of the place. These little details enrich the world-building and often provide clues for hidden items or locations.

6.2 Key Landmarks and Hidden Secrets

One of the most rewarding aspects of *Metro Awakening* is the sense of discovery. The game is packed with hidden landmarks and secrets that reward players who venture off the beaten path. Whether you're looking for powerful weapons, rare resources, or lore that deepens the story, these hidden gems are crucial for a full experience.

Hidden Landmarks

1. **The Abandoned Train Station**: A once-bustling hub now overrun by mutated creatures and scavengers. Inside, you'll find not only rare weapons and upgrades but also an eerie sense of nostalgia. The station's crumbling infrastructure and decayed trains offer a haunting glimpse into the past.

2. **The Underground Church**: Deep within the metro tunnels lies an old church, its once-pristine interior now twisted by time and decay. It's a place of reverence for the survivors, and while it offers

shelter, it also hides a number of important items, from health kits to unique artifacts.

3. **The Damaged Skyscraper**: This iconic landmark towers above the wasteland, a symbol of humanity's lost ambition. The climb to the top is treacherous, filled with mutant creatures and environmental hazards. However, reaching the summit rewards you with a breathtaking view and rare loot, including high-level weapon parts.

4. **The Radiation Zone**: One of the most dangerous locations in the game, this area is filled with deadly radiation that can quickly drain your health. However, the risk is worth it, as rare blueprints, materials, and even powerful weapons are scattered throughout the zone. Navigating the Radiation Zone requires a good strategy, proper equipment, and quick thinking.

Hidden Secrets and Collectibles

In addition to landmarks, the game is filled with collectibles that offer rich rewards. Some of the most notable include:

- **Postcards**: Scattered throughout the world are collectible postcards that not only give you insight into the world before the apocalypse but also serve as trophies. Collecting all of them unlocks a special achievement and provides a sense of accomplishment.

- **Notes and Diaries**: Exploring the environments reveals personal notes and diaries left behind by survivors, scientists, and other individuals. These give context to the game's events and shed light on the larger lore of the world. Some of these entries also contain vital clues for solving puzzles or finding hidden paths.
- **Hidden Workbenches**: Throughout the game, hidden workbenches allow you to upgrade your weapons and gear. Finding these hidden workbenches requires exploration and keen observation, as they are often tucked away in hard-to-reach places.

6.3 Navigating the Terrain: Best Practices for Survival

Surviving in *Metro Awakening* requires a combination of careful planning, resource management, and environmental awareness. The world is unforgiving, and mistakes can lead to death or wasted resources. Below are some of the best practices for navigating the harsh terrain and staying alive in this unforgiving world.

Always Be Prepared

The first rule of survival in *Metro Awakening* is always to be prepared. Whether you're traversing the metro tunnels or braving the wasteland, you need to have the right equipment and supplies. Keep a careful stock of gas mask filters, ammunition, medical supplies, and crafting materials. The game doesn't give you much room for error, and being caught without the right items could mean the difference between life and death.

Map and Navigation

While *Metro Awakening* doesn't provide a traditional map for every area, there are ways to navigate effectively. Pay attention to the layout of each area and use landmarks to orient yourself. The game's detailed environments provide plenty of clues to help you navigate, from street signs and graffiti to the remnants of collapsed structures. Many of the areas also feature light sources or glowing signs to guide you toward key objectives.

When traveling through the metro system, use the trains as checkpoints. They often mark key areas that are safe or lead to vital parts of the city. While the underground passages may seem like a maze at first, you'll soon begin to recognize familiar landmarks and routes that help you navigate more efficiently.

Utilize Stealth

In many situations, outright combat is not your best option. Instead, focus on using stealth to bypass dangerous enemies. Moving silently, using distractions, and choosing the right moment to strike or hide are all essential strategies for survival. The world of *Metro Awakening* is filled with threats, and avoiding unnecessary fights is often the best way to conserve resources and stay alive.

Watch Your Health and Stamina

In harsh environments, managing your health and stamina is critical. When exploring, always be on the lookout for medkits, food, and water sources. Health restoration is often limited, so it's important to use these items sparingly and only when absolutely necessary. Similarly, stamina is a valuable resource when running or climbing, so make sure you're not overexerting yourself unless required for survival.

Learn the Terrain and Hazards

The environment in *Metro Awakening* is filled with hidden dangers. From toxic gas and radiation zones to unstable bridges and environmental traps, the terrain can be just as lethal as the creatures that roam it. Learn the different environmental hazards in each area and take precautions to avoid them. Use your gas mask wisely and keep an eye on the filter levels when venturing into contaminated areas.

6.4 Resource Management: How to Gather and Use Supplies Effectively

In *Metro Awakening*, managing resources is crucial to survival. Whether you're scavenging for ammunition or crafting new weapons, you'll need to make every resource count. Here are some tips on how to gather and use supplies effectively.

Scavenging for Resources

The world of *Metro Awakening* is rich in resources, but they are often in limited supply. Searching for supplies in the environment is your primary method of gathering what you need to survive. Look for abandoned vehicles, destroyed buildings, and corpses of fallen enemies to scavenge for ammunition, health items, and valuable crafting materials.

Crafting and Upgrades

Crafting is an essential aspect of resource management. You can combine various materials to create new items like medkits, gas mask filters, and upgraded weapons. Keep an eye out for rare crafting components like scrap metal, wires, and chemicals, which can be used to enhance your gear or create powerful weapons.

Trading with Survivors

In some areas, survivors set up trading posts where you can exchange resources. These are great opportunities to stock up on rare supplies or purchase unique items that you can't find elsewhere. Always make sure you have enough valuable items to trade, as supplies are scarce in the wasteland.

Chapter 7: Equipment and Customization

In *Metro Awakening*, your ability to survive depends heavily on the weapons, armor, and equipment you carry. However, the game goes beyond simply handing you powerful tools—it requires that you customize, craft, and upgrade them to maximize your efficiency and effectiveness. From crafting makeshift weapons to fine-tuning your combat gear, this section provides everything you need to build the perfect arsenal for your journey through the Metro's perilous tunnels and wastelands.

Every piece of equipment can play a vital role in your survival, but making smart decisions about what to prioritize and how to customize your gear can mean the difference between life and death. The key to success lies in strategic management of your resources and a deep understanding of how different pieces of equipment complement your playstyle.

7.1 Weapons and Mods: How to Optimize Your Arsenal

The weapons in *Metro Awakening* are not just tools for survival—they are your lifeline. Whether you're facing mutated creatures, hostile factions, or environmental hazards, your weapons must be versatile, reliable, and well-optimized. However, it's not enough to simply collect weapons. You'll need to learn how to customize them with modifications (mods) to increase their efficiency, accuracy, and damage output.

Weapons Overview

In *Metro Awakening*, your arsenal consists of a mix of classic firearms, makeshift weaponry, and experimental technology. Some weapons are versatile all-rounders, while others excel in specific combat situations.

- **Pistols**: Quick, efficient, and easy to use, pistols are a great choice for stealth and close-quarters combat. They don't pack as much punch as rifles, but they are lightweight and can be easily concealed.

- **Rifles and Assault Weapons**: For longer-range engagements, rifles and assault weapons are invaluable. These weapons offer better accuracy and stopping power but often come at the cost of reload speed and mobility.

- **Shotguns**: Ideal for clearing out groups of enemies, shotguns are devastating in close quarters. However, they require more precise timing, as the spread of their shots can be inconsistent.

- **Sniper Rifles**: If you prefer a stealthy approach and want to pick off enemies from afar, sniper rifles are your best bet. These weapons offer incredible range and accuracy but leave you vulnerable when reloading or repositioning.

- **Makeshift Weapons**: In the unforgiving world of *Metro Awakening*, creativity is key. Makeshift weapons—ranging from modified tools to improvised explosives—can be used to give you an edge when ammunition is scarce.

Weapon Mods and Customization

The real magic of *Metro Awakening* lies in its weapon modding system. The ability to customize your weapons to suit your needs is a core gameplay mechanic. Mods can enhance damage, improve accuracy, reduce recoil, and even add new functionalities.

Here's a breakdown of the primary weapon mods you'll encounter and how to use them effectively:

- **Barrels**: Changing the barrel can have a huge impact on your weapon's accuracy and range. Short barrels reduce weight and recoil but lower range, while long barrels increase stability and damage but make the weapon slower to aim and reload.

- **Optics**: Optics mods, such as scopes and red-dot sights, improve your accuracy at long range. Choose optics based on your preferred playstyle—scopes for precision shooting and red-dot sights for quick target acquisition.

- **Stocks and Grips**: Adding a stock or grip to your weapon can reduce recoil and improve handling, especially for rifles and shotguns. Stocks provide better stability, making aiming more accurate, while grips help reduce the weapon's tendency to sway.

- **Suppressors**: For stealthy players, suppressors are a must. They significantly reduce the noise of your shots, allowing you to take out enemies without alerting others to your presence. Keep in mind that suppressors often reduce damage, so use them strategically.

- **Magazines**: Upgrading your magazine increases the capacity of your weapon's ammunition, meaning fewer reloads during a firefight. Larger magazines are ideal for situations where you're up against multiple enemies.

- **Triggers**: A quick-trigger mod can help with faster firing rates. While this can be useful in close combat, it often reduces accuracy, so it's best to use it on weapons with high damage but slower firing speeds, like rifles.

Optimizing Your Arsenal

To make the most of your weapons and mods, it's essential to consider your preferred combat style and tailor your loadout accordingly.

- **Stealth Playstyle**: If you're relying on stealth, choose suppressed weapons with optics for long-range engagement. A silenced pistol or compact rifle can be invaluable in taking out enemies quietly. Always ensure that your mods focus on minimizing noise and maximizing stealth.

- **Run-and-Gun Playstyle**: For a more aggressive playstyle, opt for weapons with high rate-of-fire and large magazines. Assault rifles or shotguns are perfect for clearing rooms, while mods that enhance recoil control will ensure you don't lose accuracy in the heat of combat.

- **Sniper Playstyle**: If sniping is your preference, make sure your sniper rifle is equipped with high-powered optics and a stock that enhances stability. Consider mods that reduce sway and improve range to ensure you can eliminate targets from long distances.

7.2 Armor and Protective Gear

In the dangerous world of *Metro Awakening*, armor and protective gear are just as important as weapons. Without proper protection, even the most skilled player can be overwhelmed by the game's fierce enemies, environmental hazards, and traps. Armor comes in a variety of forms, from light body armor to heavy suits designed for extreme conditions.

Types of Armor

1. **Light Armor**: Light armor is designed for players who prefer mobility. It offers minimal protection against damage but allows you to move quickly and stealthily. Ideal for players who want to avoid taking hits altogether and focus on avoiding combat.

2. **Medium Armor**: The middle ground between mobility and protection, medium armor offers a balanced approach. It provides decent protection from gunfire and melee attacks while still allowing for reasonable movement. This is the most versatile armor type for players who want to stay agile while being able to take a few hits.

3. **Heavy Armor**: Heavy armor offers the best protection, shielding you from the most dangerous attacks. However, it comes with a significant drawback—reduced mobility. Heavy armor severely limits your ability to move quickly or stealthily, so it's most effective when you're facing heavily armed enemies or engaging in prolonged firefights.

Protective Gear and Environmental Suit

In addition to body armor, *Metro Awakening* introduces specialized protective gear to help you survive in extreme environments.

- **Gas Mask**: Perhaps the most iconic piece of gear in the *Metro* series, the gas mask is essential for surviving in the radioactive wasteland and contaminated metro tunnels. Be sure to stock up on gas mask filters, as their lifespan is limited. Running out of filters in hazardous areas can be deadly.

- **Hazard Suits**: Some areas in the game feature dangerous environmental hazards such as toxic fumes, extreme radiation, or intense heat. A hazard suit offers protection against these environmental dangers. Always keep an eye on the durability of your suit and look for safe zones where you can rest and repair your equipment.

- **Heat-Resistant Gear**: In specific parts of the game, you'll encounter extreme temperatures. Heat-resistant gear helps protect you from the dangerous heat of certain areas, preventing your health from draining too quickly.

Upgrading Armor

Armor upgrades are often less visible than weapon mods but just as essential for survival. As you progress through the game, you'll gain access to upgrade stations where you can enhance your armor and protective gear. Upgrades can provide you with:

- **Increased durability**: Reduces the amount of damage your armor takes before it needs repair.

- **Resistance to specific damage types**: Upgrades can make you more resistant to specific threats like fire, radiation, or explosive damage.

- **Stealth upgrades**: Some upgrades reduce your armor's noise level, making it less likely to alert enemies when you're sneaking around.

By customizing your armor, you can ensure that you're prepared for whatever the world of *Metro Awakening* throws at you.

7.3 Crafting and Resource Management

Crafting is an integral part of *Metro Awakening*. Resources are scarce, and you'll need to be resourceful in order to survive. Whether you're creating new weapons, crafting health kits, or upgrading your equipment, effective resource management is the key to maintaining your survivability.

Crafting Materials

In *Metro Awakening*, you'll collect various materials as you explore the world. These materials can be found in abandoned vehicles, structures, or taken from fallen enemies. The primary materials you'll need include:

- **Metal scraps**: Used to craft weapon mods, ammunition, and repairs.
- **Chemicals**: Vital for crafting health kits and other consumables.
- **Fabric and leather**: Needed for creating armor and protective gear.
- **Weapon parts**: Essential for upgrading and modifying your arsenal.

Crafting Workbenches

Throughout the game, you'll find crafting stations known as **workbenches**. These stations allow you to craft new items or upgrade existing equipment. It's important to prioritize crafting health kits, gas mask filters, and ammo early on, as these are often the most important resources in the game.

Resource Management Tips

1. **Prioritize essentials**: Always keep a stock of medkits, filters, and ammunition. If you find yourself low on any of these resources, prioritize crafting or scavenging for them.

2. **Don't overstock**: While it's tempting to hoard every piece of scrap metal or fabric, it's important to balance your resources. Carry only what you need, as your inventory space is limited.

3. **Use the environment**: Look for environmental objects that can be scavenged. Items like old vehicles and broken buildings often contain useful materials for crafting.

7.4 Upgrades and Enhancements: Maximizing Efficiency

Upgrades are not just about enhancing the effectiveness of your weapons or armor—they're about maximizing your efficiency in combat and exploration. The more you upgrade, the easier it becomes to navigate the world and overcome its many challenges.

Weapon Upgrades

Weapon upgrades are crucial for staying competitive. Some of the most important upgrades include:

- **Damage increases**: Maximize the damage output of your favorite weapons to deal with tougher enemies more easily.

- **Accuracy mods**: Perfect for long-range weapons, mods that increase accuracy ensure you can hit distant targets with precision.

- **Reload speed**: When under fire, reload speed can be the difference between life and death. Consider upgrading this stat for weapons that require frequent reloading.

Armor Upgrades

Just as you can upgrade weapons, you can also enhance your armor to improve its durability and resistance. Prioritize armor upgrades that will protect you from the specific dangers in each area.

Chapter 8: VR Mode: Immersion and Tips

Playing *Metro Awakening* in virtual reality offers an entirely new level of immersion. The deep, atmospheric world of *Metro* is designed to be experienced up close and personal, with VR giving players the ability to truly feel like they're navigating the treacherous metro tunnels, battling mutated horrors, and surviving in a world filled with danger. However, VR gaming also presents unique challenges, from setup to physical comfort. In this section, we'll guide you through everything you need to know to enjoy the best possible VR experience, including what to expect, how to set up your VR system, and tips for enhancing your gameplay.

8.1 The VR Experience: What to Expect

When you enter the world of *Metro Awakening* through virtual reality, the first thing you'll notice is how much more intimate the experience feels. The game's signature atmosphere of tension, survival, and discovery comes alive like never before. With VR, you'll have a full 360-degree field of view, a heightened sense of spatial awareness, and an immersive first-person perspective that makes the game world seem more real and immediate.

Visuals and Immersion

One of the most significant differences in VR is the visual fidelity and depth of field. With the immersive view, you'll be able to look around freely, physically moving your head to interact with your environment. This adds a natural layer of depth and believability that traditional gaming can't replicate. The feeling of physically being in the Metro tunnels, glancing over your shoulder at unseen threats, or looking down to inspect your gear is a level of immersion that VR uniquely offers.

- **Exploration**: The sense of scale is incredible in VR. When you walk through abandoned metro stations or take cover behind crumbling walls, you'll feel as though you're truly there. The game's art direction—rich with atmospheric lighting, detailed environments, and dense fog—becomes even more impressive in VR. The corridors seem narrower, the darkness deeper, and the danger closer.

- **Combat**: Combat is another area where VR excels. The tension of aiming down sights with your rifle, the panic of reloading in the middle of a firefight, and the satisfaction of taking out enemies from a distance all come to life in VR. Whether you're engaging in intense firefights or using stealth to outwit your foes, every encounter feels more visceral in virtual reality.

- **Environmental Interactions**: One of the more exciting aspects of VR in *Metro Awakening* is the ability to interact with objects more naturally. Reaching out to grab an item, manually reloading your weapon, or adjusting your gas mask all require physical movements that further add to the realism. The more you explore, the more you'll appreciate how VR enhances your connection to the world around you.

Sound Design and Spatial Audio

In addition to the visual experience, the sound design in VR is crucial for building immersion. The game's detailed spatial audio, combined with the head-tracking capabilities of VR, allows you to detect the location of enemies and environmental sounds in a more lifelike way. The subtle creaks of distant creatures, the rush of water in the sewers, or the eerie echoes in abandoned metro stations will surround you, making you feel as if you're truly part of the world.

8.2 Setting Up and Adjusting for VR Play

To get the most out of your VR experience, it's important to ensure that your VR system is set up correctly and that your game settings are optimized. The setup process can vary depending on the VR headset you're using, but the following general guidelines will help you get started.

Hardware Requirements

Before diving into the setup, make sure your system meets the hardware requirements for VR play. A high-performance PC with a capable graphics card (such as the Nvidia RTX 3060 or better) is recommended, as VR gaming requires substantial power to maintain a smooth experience. Additionally, ensure that your VR headset is compatible with your system.

- **VR Headsets**: Popular VR headsets like the Oculus Rift S, HTC Vive Pro, or the Valve Index are great choices for immersive gameplay in *Metro Awakening*. Each headset has its unique features, but they all offer the basic VR experiences such as head tracking, hand controllers, and spatial audio.

- **Controller Setup**: Your VR controllers will be essential for navigation and combat in *Metro Awakening*. Make sure they're properly synced with your VR system. Familiarize yourself with the button layout and customize it to fit your playstyle. Controllers with haptic feedback can also enhance the immersion, making combat feel even more real.

Play Area Setup

Before you start playing, make sure your play area is safe and spacious enough to accommodate the movements required by the game. VR games like *Metro Awakening* often involve physical movement—whether you're ducking behind cover, reloading your weapon, or physically dodging attacks.

- **Clear the Area**: Remove obstacles from your play area to prevent accidental bumps or injuries. Ideally, you should have at least a 6x6-foot space for safe movement.

- **Safety Boundaries**: Set up your VR system's boundary system (such as the Guardian boundary on Oculus devices or Chaperone on Vive headsets) to alert you when you're about to step out of your play area. This will help avoid collisions with furniture or walls while you're deeply immersed in the game.

Adjusting Game Settings for VR

Once you've set up your hardware and play area, it's time to adjust the game's settings for optimal performance and comfort.

- **Field of View (FOV)**: In VR, your field of view is crucial for immersion. Ensure that *Metro Awakening* is set to the optimal FOV setting. A wider FOV can help you see more of your surroundings and provide better situational awareness.

- **Comfort Settings**: VR gaming can sometimes cause discomfort, especially if you're new to it. *Metro Awakening* offers several comfort options, such as reducing motion blur, enabling comfort mode, or allowing smooth turning. Adjusting these settings can help reduce nausea or disorientation, especially during intense sequences.

- **Performance Settings**: VR gaming demands a high frame rate to ensure a smooth experience. Set your graphics options to match your system's capabilities. Lowering certain graphical settings, like texture resolution or shadow quality, can significantly improve performance without sacrificing immersion.

- **Adjusting Height and Calibration**: It's important to calibrate your VR system for your height. This ensures that your character's viewpoint aligns correctly with the environment. Most VR systems will allow you to set your height by standing up straight during calibration.

8.3 Tips for Enhancing VR Gameplay

To make your VR experience even more enjoyable, here are some essential tips to enhance your gameplay in *Metro Awakening*:

1. Take Breaks Regularly

VR can be physically demanding, especially during long gaming sessions. It's important to take regular breaks to avoid eye strain, dizziness, or discomfort. Stand up, stretch, and give your eyes a rest from the headset every 30 minutes or so. This will help prevent VR fatigue and keep you feeling fresh throughout your play session.

2. Experiment with Comfort Options

Every player's tolerance to VR is different. Some players may experience motion sickness or dizziness, especially in fast-moving sequences. *Metro Awakening* offers various comfort settings, such as reduced motion blur, snap turning, or vignette effects, to help minimize discomfort.

Experiment with these settings until you find the combination that works best for you.

3. Use a VR-Ready Chair or Standing Setup

Depending on your preferred playstyle, you can play *Metro Awakening* either seated or standing. If you prefer standing, make sure you have enough space to move freely. Alternatively, if you're playing seated, use a comfortable VR-ready chair that allows you to turn, crouch, and reload your weapons without restriction. A chair can also help provide stability and balance during intense combat sequences.

4. Immerse Yourself with Surround Sound

Good sound is crucial for full immersion, and VR amplifies the impact of spatial audio. If you're using a VR headset with integrated audio, make sure to adjust the volume for clarity without overwhelming the senses. If your headset doesn't have built-in audio, consider using high-quality headphones to enhance the environmental sound and enemy audio cues.

5. Familiarize Yourself with Motion Controls

In VR, you'll interact with the game world using hand controllers. Familiarize yourself with the motion control mechanics early on. Practice actions like grabbing, reloading, and aiming down sights. Being comfortable with these controls will help make the transition to VR smoother and less stressful during tense moments.

6. Adjust the Lighting

Lighting plays a major role in both the game's atmosphere and your comfort in VR. Ensure that your room has proper lighting—neither too dark nor too bright. Excessive light can cause glare on your VR headset, while a completely dark room might make you feel disoriented. A balanced lighting setup will help reduce eye strain and improve visibility during gameplay.

8.4 Overcoming VR Challenges and Comfort Issues

While VR is an incredibly immersive way to experience *Metro Awakening*, it can also introduce some challenges, especially for players who are new to VR or those who experience discomfort. Here are some tips for overcoming common VR challenges:

Motion Sickness

Motion sickness is one of the most common issues in VR, particularly when moving quickly or when there's a disconnect between your physical movement and what you see in the game.

- **Comfort Modes**: As mentioned earlier, many VR systems offer comfort settings that can reduce motion sickness. Enable these settings, including teleportation movement or smooth turning, to reduce disorientation.
- **Shorter Play Sessions**: Gradually increase your playtime in VR to build tolerance. Start with shorter

sessions, and over time, your body will adapt to the sensation of movement in virtual reality.

- **Look at a Fixed Point**: When navigating, try focusing on a fixed point ahead of you. This can help your brain reconcile the movement in the game world with the stillness of your physical body.

Eye Strain and Fatigue

Extended VR play can lead to eye strain, especially if you're playing for long hours. Adjust the distance between the lenses and your eyes to ensure a comfortable fit. Also, take breaks every 30 minutes to rest your eyes and reduce strain.

Chapter 9: Advanced Strategies and Endgame Content

In *Metro Awakening*, the journey doesn't end when you complete the main storyline. The true challenge begins as you dive into the advanced strategies required to fully optimize your character, conquer the most difficult missions, and discover hidden secrets that enhance replayability. This section is dedicated to those players who want to push their skills to the limit, get the most out of the endgame content, and explore every facet of the game that *Metro Awakening* has to offer.

9.1 Maximizing Your Character Build

By the time you reach the late stages of *Metro Awakening*, your character's abilities, equipment, and skills should reflect the challenges you'll face in the toughest missions. Perfecting your character build is key to surviving these high-stakes encounters and achieving 100% completion in the game. Below, we'll break down the best ways to maximize your build, focusing on key areas such as abilities, gear, and combat strategies.

Choosing Your Playstyle

The first step in optimizing your character is determining your preferred playstyle. *Metro Awakening* offers a range of skills and abilities, allowing you to tailor your character's strengths to your needs. The two primary playstyles you can choose from are:

1. **Stealth Playstyle**: If you prefer to avoid direct confrontation, focusing on stealth and subterfuge is essential. Invest heavily in abilities that enhance your movement speed, silence, and distractions. Skills that help you disable traps and enemies without alerting others will be crucial, as well as those that allow you to craft silent weapons like the crossbow.

2. **Combat Playstyle**: For those who prefer direct combat, maximizing your offensive abilities is paramount. Focus on increasing your proficiency with firearms, armor, and damage resistance. Prioritize abilities that enhance reload speeds, damage output, and critical hits. Additionally, boosting your stamina and health will allow you to withstand extended firefights.

3. **Balanced Playstyle**: The most versatile approach is a hybrid one. A balanced build will allow you to switch between stealth and direct combat depending on the situation. Invest in abilities that support both, such as those that improve detection resistance, increase combat efficiency, and expand your arsenal of tools and weapons.

Optimizing Skill Trees

Each playstyle will have a specific skill tree with various branches of progression. Here are the key areas to focus on:

- **Stealth Skills**: These are essential for sneaking past enemies, avoiding detection, and disabling traps. Skills like "Silent Movement," "Deceptive Distractions," and "Shadow Step" make it possible to bypass enemies without firing a single shot. These are perfect for players who enjoy a tactical approach to combat.

- **Combat Skills**: Players who prefer to engage enemies head-on should focus on improving gunplay and survivability. Look for skills like "Adept Marksman" (improving accuracy), "Quick Reflexes" (enhancing your ability to dodge attacks), and "Tank" (increasing your health and armor resistance). These abilities will increase your efficiency in combat and give you an edge in firefights.

- **Crafting and Resource Management**: Whether you're focused on combat or stealth, managing your resources efficiently is key. Upgrade crafting and scavenging skills to ensure you always have the materials you need for ammunition, health packs, and other essential gear. The more resources you can gather and craft, the longer you can survive in the harsh world of *Metro Awakening*.

Perfecting Your Arsenal

Weapons are vital to your survival, and your arsenal should reflect your character build. Here's a breakdown of how to choose the best weapons for your chosen playstyle:

- **For Stealth**: The crossbow, silenced pistol, and melee weapons like knives are ideal for stealth builds. The crossbow is a particularly powerful tool for silently taking out enemies from a distance without alerting others. Additionally, a silenced SMG or handgun can help you remain undetected while dispatching foes quietly.

- **For Combat**: If you're a fan of going all-out in firefights, focus on powerful assault rifles, shotguns, and sniper rifles. The assault rifle offers versatility for close-quarters combat and longer-range engagements, while the shotgun excels at devastating foes up close. The sniper rifle, on the other hand, provides superior range and accuracy, ideal for picking off enemies from afar.

- **For a Balanced Build**: A balanced player should carry a variety of weapons to adapt to any situation. Carrying a close-quarters weapon like a shotgun or melee weapon, alongside a longer-range rifle or crossbow, will provide you with the flexibility to switch between stealth and combat as needed.

9.2 Endgame Strategies for the Most Difficult Missions

Once you've completed the main story, you'll unlock some of the toughest challenges in *Metro Awakening*. These missions require a high level of preparation, patience, and strategic thinking. Here are a few essential strategies for taking on the hardest content in the game:

1. Know the Terrain

The endgame missions in *Metro Awakening* often take place in complex, hostile environments. Understanding the layout of the area and the positioning of enemies is crucial. Before jumping into combat, take the time to explore and survey the area. Look for chokepoints, hidden passages, and environmental hazards that you can use to your advantage. Additionally, knowing where to find resources like medkits, ammo, and crafting materials will help you stay prepared for the hardest battles.

2. Optimize Ammo and Resources

In the toughest endgame encounters, ammunition is often scarce, and resources become even more vital. Stockpile materials and craft ammo whenever possible. Be sure to carry a variety of weapon types to adapt to different combat situations, and always make sure you have a full supply of healing items.

- **Crafting Supplies**: Look for crafting stations in key areas and gather supplies for making medkits, ammo, and traps. Keep an eye out for scrap materials, as they can be used to create powerful upgrades for your gear.

- **Managing Ammo**: Don't waste precious rounds on weaker enemies. Conserve ammo for difficult boss fights or large groups of enemies. Prioritize headshots for higher damage output and efficiency.

3. Take Advantage of Environmental Hazards

One of the most satisfying ways to defeat enemies in the late stages of the game is to use the environment to your advantage. Many endgame locations are filled with explosive barrels, traps, and other hazards. Learn how to trigger environmental hazards to cause massive damage to enemies while minimizing your own risk. Use stealth to place enemies near explosive containers, or lure them into traps that will disable or kill them.

4. Stay Agile and Aware

In endgame missions, you'll often face overwhelming odds. The best strategy is to stay nimble and be prepared to adapt. Move quickly between cover, keep track of enemy positions, and always be ready to retreat if necessary. Stay aware of your surroundings and use every tool at your disposal to outwit and outmaneuver the enemy.

9.3 Collectibles and Achievements

The endgame content in *Metro Awakening* is packed with hidden collectibles and achievements that add replay value and depth to the experience. Completing these objectives is not only satisfying but will unlock various bonuses, such as new weapons, skins, and game modes.

Collectibles

Metro Awakening features a variety of collectibles scattered throughout the game world. These items include:

- **Artifacts**: Rare items that can be found hidden in hard-to-reach places or after defeating difficult enemies. Some artifacts provide useful boosts to your character's abilities or unlock special bonuses.

- **Documents and Logs**: Collecting documents, journals, and audio logs will provide deeper insight into the game's story and lore, helping you uncover hidden secrets and the backstory of key locations and characters.

Achievements

The game also offers a wide range of achievements for players who want to complete every challenge. These achievements may involve defeating difficult bosses, completing the game on higher difficulty levels, or finding all collectibles. Earning these achievements will not only show your mastery of the game but also unlock special rewards.

9.4 New Game+ and Replay Value

One of the most exciting features of *Metro Awakening* is its New Game+ mode, which allows you to replay the game with all your progress carried over. This mode is perfect for those who want to explore different character builds, experiment with alternate strategies, or unlock all the collectibles and achievements.

What's New in New Game+

- **Increased Difficulty**: Enemies will be tougher, and resources will be scarcer, making New Game+ an even greater challenge. It's the perfect opportunity to test your character build and apply everything you've learned.

- **Unlockables**: New Game+ unlocks additional story content, secret weapons, and special gear that you can carry over into your next playthrough. This mode is ideal for players who want to see everything the game has to offer and push their skills to the limit.

Replay Value

The game's open-ended nature and multiple difficulty levels mean that there's a lot of replay value to be found. Whether you're looking to experiment with different character builds, explore all the side missions, or hunt down every collectible, *Metro Awakening* offers endless opportunities for replay. Each new playthrough can offer a fresh challenge and a different experience, making it a game that's worth revisiting time and time again.

you're now ready to tackle the game's most difficult content and enjoy everything *Metro Awakening* has to offer in its entirety.

Chapter 10:

Troubleshooting and FAQs

No game is perfect, and *Metro Awakening* is no exception. As players dive deeper into the game, they may encounter some common issues or have questions about certain aspects of gameplay. This section will provide you with solutions to some of the most frequently encountered problems and offer answers to common questions that players have during their journey. Additionally, we'll discuss how to reach out for community and developer support in case the issue persists.

10.1 Common Issues and Fixes

While *Metro Awakening* has been optimized for a smooth experience, players may still run into a few bugs, performance issues, or settings-related problems. Here's a list of some of the most common problems and how to fix them.

1. Game Crashing or Freezing

Issue: The game may crash or freeze during loading screens or gameplay.

Fix: This issue can occur due to outdated graphics drivers or insufficient system resources. Here's how to resolve it:

- **Update Graphics Drivers**: Ensure that your GPU drivers are up to date. Visit the official website of your graphics card manufacturer (NVIDIA, AMD, or Intel) to download the latest drivers.

- **Check System Requirements**: Double-check that your system meets or exceeds the minimum requirements for *Metro Awakening*. If your hardware is close to the minimum, reducing the game's graphics settings might help.

- **Verify Game Files**: If you're playing on Steam, use the "Verify Integrity of Game Files" option to check if any files are corrupted or missing.

- **Close Background Programs**: Close any unnecessary background programs that might be consuming system resources.

2. Low FPS (Frames Per Second) or Lag

Issue: The game may run at a lower FPS than expected, causing stuttering or lag during gameplay.

Fix: Low FPS or lag can often be attributed to graphics settings, background processes, or hardware limitations. Here are some steps to improve performance:

- **Lower Graphics Settings**: Go to the game's settings menu and lower the graphical settings such as texture quality, shadows, and anti-aliasing. Disabling V-Sync or reducing the resolution can also help.

- **Enable Performance Mode**: On PC, make sure that your system is running in performance mode (rather than power-saving mode) in the power settings.

- **Close Unnecessary Background Apps**: Ensure that no resource-heavy applications (e.g., web browsers, video players, etc.) are running in the background, as they may be affecting your game's performance.

- **Upgrade Your Hardware**: If you continue to experience performance issues despite lowering settings, it may be time to consider upgrading your PC's GPU, CPU, or adding more RAM.

3. Audio Issues (No Sound or Glitches)

Issue: The game may experience audio problems such as no sound or distorted audio during gameplay.

Fix: Audio issues can stem from several factors, such as incorrect audio settings or conflicts with your sound drivers.

- **Check In-Game Audio Settings**: Ensure that the game's audio settings are configured correctly. Verify that sound levels (master volume, music, effects, etc.) are not set to zero.

- **Update Audio Drivers**: Visit the website of your sound card or motherboard manufacturer to check for updated audio drivers.

- **Check System Audio Settings**: Make sure your system's audio settings are properly configured. Right-click the volume icon in your system tray, select "Playback Devices," and ensure the correct output device (headphones, speakers, etc.) is selected.

- **Restart the Game or System**: Sometimes, restarting the game or even rebooting your computer can resolve audio issues.

- **Try Alternate Output Devices**: If you're using headphones or external speakers, try switching to a different output device to see if the issue persists.

4. Controller Not Working (PC)

Issue: If you're playing on PC with a controller, it may not be recognized or may malfunction.

Fix: The game supports a wide variety of controllers, but sometimes they may not be detected due to settings or software conflicts.

- **Check Controller Settings**: Go to the game's settings menu and ensure that your controller is selected as the input device.

- **Install or Update Drivers**: Make sure your controller's drivers are up to date. If you're using an Xbox or PlayStation controller, check if the latest drivers are installed on your PC.

- **Use Steam Big Picture Mode**: If you're using Steam, try launching *Metro Awakening* through Big Picture Mode, which offers more stable controller support.

- **Disconnect Other Input Devices**: If you have multiple input devices (keyboard, mouse, etc.) connected to your PC, disconnect them temporarily to avoid conflicts.

5. Save File Issues (Corrupt or Missing Saves)

Issue: Some players report issues with save files becoming corrupted or not appearing.

Fix: To resolve save file issues, follow these steps:

- **Check Save Location**: Ensure your save files are being stored in the correct location on your hard drive. If you're using Steam, check the cloud storage settings.

- **Backup Your Saves**: Regularly back up your save files, especially before making any major system changes or updates. Save files are usually stored in the "Documents" or "AppData" folders on your PC.

- **Verify Game Files**: If the game is crashing or you suspect missing files, use the Steam client to verify the integrity of your game files.

- **Restart from a Previous Save**: If your save file becomes corrupted, you may need to revert to an earlier save. Look for any autosave files or manual backups you've created.

- **Use Cloud Saves**: Steam offers cloud saving for games that support it. Make sure the cloud save feature is enabled, which can help recover lost saves in some instances.

10.2 Frequently Asked Questions

Q1: How do I unlock New Game+ mode?

A: New Game+ becomes available once you complete the main story. After finishing the game, you will be given the option to start a New Game+ playthrough, where you can carry over all of your character's abilities, gear, and progress.

Q2: How do I find all collectibles?

A: Collectibles are scattered across the game world and can be found in both main story missions and side content. Look for hidden rooms, off-path areas, and explore thoroughly to uncover all the collectibles. Some of them are tied to achievements, so if you're going for 100% completion, keep an eye out for every detail.

Q3: Can I change my character build during the game?

A: While you cannot completely reset your skill points or gear mid-playthrough, there are ways to adjust your build. You can find special respec items later in the game that allow you to redistribute your skill points, which can help if you want to switch your character's focus from stealth to combat, for example.

Q4: How do I increase my inventory space?

A: Your inventory space can be expanded by upgrading your gear through crafting. As you progress through the game, you will unlock more crafting options that allow you to carry more items, such as ammo, medkits, and resources.

Q5: Why are my achievements not unlocking?

A: Sometimes, achievements may not unlock due to bugs or glitches. If you're sure you've met the criteria, try restarting the game, or checking the Steam or platform store for updates. You can also check online forums or developer patch notes for any known issues with specific achievements.

10.3 Community and Developer Support

If you continue to experience issues or have questions that this guide hasn't addressed, you can reach out to the *Metro Awakening* community and developers for support. Here's how to get help:

1. Community Forums
Join the official *Metro Awakening* forums or community spaces to get support from fellow players. These forums are a great place to discuss problems, share tips, and ask questions. The community is often very active, and many experienced players are willing to help troubleshoot issues.

- **Official Forums**: Metro Awakening Community Forum

- **Reddit**: Subreddits like r/MetroAwakening are full of players sharing their experiences and solutions to common problems.

2. Developer Support
If you can't find a solution in the forums, you can contact the developers for direct assistance. The official support team will help you troubleshoot more complicated issues, such as missing files, technical errors, or bugs.

- **Contact Support**: Visit the official *Metro Awakening* website and use the support page to submit a help request. Make sure to provide details about the issue you're encountering and your system specifications.
- **Social media**: You can also reach out via social media platforms such as Twitter, Facebook, or Discord, where the developers actively interact with the community.

3. Patches and Updates
Keep your game up-to-date by downloading the latest patches and updates, which often fix bugs and improve performance. Check for updates regularly, especially after encountering any issues.

- **Patch Notes**: The official website and forums often post patch notes detailing bug fixes and known issues. These notes can help you determine whether a problem you're experiencing has already been addressed.

With the information in this section, you should be equipped to handle most common issues and continue enjoying *Metro Awakening*. Whether you're troubleshooting technical problems or seeking help from the community, you'll find that there are plenty of resources available to ensure a smooth and enjoyable experience.

Conclusion

As you've worked your way through this comprehensive guide, you've gained the tools and knowledge necessary to tackle every challenge *Metro Awakening* throws your way. Whether you're a seasoned veteran of the *Metro* series or a newcomer to the franchise, this game has something to offer every type of player. From exploration and survival to character progression and strategic combat, *Metro Awakening* builds on the rich lore and atmospheric world of its predecessors while introducing exciting new mechanics and features that take the experience to the next level.

Let's take a moment to recap the most important aspects of the game that will help ensure you have a successful journey through the post-apocalyptic world of *Metro Awakening*. We'll also offer some final tips for conquering the game's most difficult sections and discuss what the future holds for this ever-evolving series.

11.1 Recap of Key Insights

Throughout this guide, we've broken down the core elements of *Metro Awakening* that players need to master in order to survive and thrive in its challenging world. Here's a recap of the key insights that will help you maximize your experience:

1. **Immersive Storytelling and Atmosphere**: One of the standout features of *Metro Awakening* is its deep and immersive narrative. The world is dark, atmospheric, and rich in detail, and understanding

its lore will give you a deeper connection to the characters and events unfolding around you. From the factions vying for control of the wasteland to the strange and deadly creatures lurking in the shadows, every element of the game's world is designed to pull you in.

2. **Character Customization and Development**: The protagonist's skill tree and character progression are vital to your success. As you navigate the game's various missions, you'll want to focus on upgrading abilities that complement your playstyle, whether that's stealth, combat, or survival skills. Additionally, the choices you make during character progression impact not only combat effectiveness but also your interactions with other characters in the game.

3. **Survival Mechanics and Resource Management**: The harsh environment of *Metro Awakening* demands that you constantly manage your resources. Whether it's ammunition, crafting materials, or health supplies, being mindful of what you carry and how you use your resources will be the difference between life and death. Scavenge everything you can, and never underestimate the value of a well-timed upgrade or health pack.

4. **Exploration and Environmental Mastery**: The world of *Metro Awakening* is vast, with a myriad of hidden locations, collectibles, and key landmarks scattered across the map. Learning to navigate the terrain efficiently, understanding the layout of each

region, and discovering hidden secrets are crucial to making progress. Remember to explore off the beaten path—there's often something valuable waiting for you just around the corner.

5. **Combat Strategies and Stealth**: Combat in *Metro Awakening* can be unforgiving, but it's not always about brute force. The game offers a variety of stealth options, distractions, and environmental interactions that allow you to avoid conflict or take down enemies without raising alarms. The more you learn about the enemies and environments you face, the better your chances of surviving.

6. **VR Mode**: For those playing in VR, the immersive experience is nothing short of spectacular. Whether you're exploring the dilapidated ruins of the old world or fighting for your life in close-quarters combat, the VR mode offers a level of immersion that heightens the tension and excitement of every encounter. Make sure to adjust your settings to maximize comfort and performance while playing in VR, and take breaks if you start to feel fatigued.

7. **Endgame and Replay Value**: Once you've finished the main story, *Metro Awakening* opens up even more challenges with the New Game+ mode, harder difficulty settings, and numerous collectibles and achievements to unlock. Endgame content offers hours of additional gameplay, making it a rewarding experience for players who are determined to fully explore every corner of the

game. Plus, with the potential for future DLC expansions, the game promises to evolve over time, giving you even more content to enjoy.

11.2 Final Tips for Conquering Metro Awakening

As you prepare to embark on your journey through the unforgiving world of *Metro Awakening*, here are a few final tips to help you conquer the game's toughest challenges and enjoy a smoother, more rewarding experience:

1. **Master Stealth Early On**: Stealth is often your best option for survival, especially early in the game when you have limited resources. Focus on upgrading stealth-related abilities early on and make use of distractions to avoid detection. The fewer enemies you engage directly, the better your chances of surviving.

2. **Always Keep an Eye on Your Resources**: Resources are scarce in *Metro Awakening*, so it's essential to always keep an eye on your supplies. Don't waste ammo unless absolutely necessary, and always check your surroundings for scavenging opportunities. Upgrade your inventory space as soon as possible to maximize the number of supplies you can carry.

3. **Explore Every Nook and Cranny**: Hidden collectibles and upgrades are scattered across the world, and often, they're tucked away in hard-to-reach places. Exploration is key to unlocking the full

potential of your character and discovering useful items that will help you along the way.

4. **Experiment with Different Weapons and Mods**: There's a wide array of weapons in the game, each with its own strengths and weaknesses. Try experimenting with different loadouts and mods to find what works best for you. Remember, a weapon that might seem weak at first can become a game-changer once properly modified.

5. **Don't Rush the Main Story**: While it can be tempting to rush through the main missions, remember that *Metro Awakening* is designed to be explored at your own pace. Take your time, explore side missions, and enjoy the world. The story will unfold naturally, and you'll be better prepared for the tougher challenges ahead if you've taken the time to upgrade your character and gear.

6. **Take Advantage of the Environment**: The environments in *Metro Awakening* are designed not just for exploration but also for combat. Use the terrain to your advantage, whether it's finding high ground for better sightlines or using obstacles as cover. You can even use environmental hazards like fire or toxic waste to take down enemies.

7. **Adjust Your Playstyle Based on the Situation**: Sometimes stealth is the way to go, while other times you'll need to fight your way out of a tough situation. Be ready to adapt your strategy based on the enemies you encounter and the circumstances

at hand. Flexibility in combat and exploration will give you the edge in tough scenarios.

11.3 Looking Forward: Future DLCs and Updates

While *Metro Awakening* is already a complete and thrilling game, the journey is far from over. The developers have promised several updates and downloadable content (DLC) expansions that will further expand the world and add new challenges. Here's a look at what's to come:

1. **New Story Content**: Expect new story missions that delve deeper into the lore of *Metro Awakening*. These updates will bring additional plotlines, characters, and twists that build upon the existing narrative, offering fresh experiences for players who've already completed the main game.

2. **New Playable Areas**: The game world is vast, but there's always room for more. Future DLCs are likely to introduce entirely new regions to explore, each with its own unique environments, dangers, and rewards. Whether it's a new part of the metro tunnels or a previously unexplored surface area, expect exciting new places to discover.

3. **New Weapons and Gear**: The developers have hinted at additional weapons and gear to further customize your playthrough. These additions will provide new combat options, allowing you to better tailor your character's loadout to your playstyle.

4. **Tougher Difficulty Modes**: For players who have mastered the game and are seeking an even greater challenge, the developers are expected to release new difficulty levels. These modes will increase the difficulty of enemy encounters, provide new mechanics, and introduce more complex puzzles and survival elements.

5. **Community-Driven Content**: The community around *Metro Awakening* is passionate and creative. Future DLCs may feature content inspired by player feedback, including new gameplay features, side missions, or even community-designed levels. Keep an eye on the official forums and social media channels for updates.

www.ingramcontent.com/pod-product-compliance
Lightning Source LLC
Chambersburg PA
CBHW071412220526
45469CB00004B/1264